The Adventures of
Mosquito Majeski
and Silly Stuff

Carlene A. Lanier

NEWMAN SPRINGS PUBLISHING
320 Broad Street
Red Bank, NJ 07701

First originally published by Newman Springs Publishing 2023

ISBN 978-1-68498-020-8 (Paperback)
ISBN 978-1-68498-021-5 (Digital)

Printed in the United States of America

Contents

Introduction

Hi! My name is Carlene. I was born in my grandparents' farmhouse in Arnott, Wisconsin. Arnott is a village a few miles from Stevens Point. Dad; Mom; my older brother, Bernard; and I lived there for about three years. It was a wonderful place. At the farm, we had lots of things to see and do.

Grandma Kate let me help her feed the chickens. When the hens were busy eating, we went into the chicken house to collect their eggs. That was fun.

We walked to the barn so that Grandma could milk the cows. *Splat!* "Grandma! My face is dirty!" I fussed.

She laughed and said, "I'll wash you up in the kitchen." That was how I learned milk came from cows.

When we walked up the steps to the house, a good smell came from the kitchen. Grandma had homemade bread baking in the oven! Grandma washed my face, and I sat down. When the bread was cool enough to eat, it tasted super with butter and strawberry jam spread all over it. She always had cakes, pies, and cookies in her pantry. I liked to look at all the rows of canned fruit and vegetables on the shelves too. The food looked yummy, and all of the colors were pretty. I liked almost everything in there!

Sometimes, it was fun to have someone push me on the swing, which hung from a huge tree in the front yard. In summertime, Grandpa would put me on his pony and lead it around the barnyard. At Christmastime, the pony was hitched up to a one-horse open sleigh. There were silver bells that hung on the pony's harness. The jingling sound was so cool! We sang songs when we rode around the farm. I liked to sing "Jingle Bells," and it didn't matter what time of the year it was. The little pony's feet went *clippity-clop*, and his tail went *swish-swish*.

One day, Dad told my grandparents that he was going to work for the Soo Line Railroad. That meant we would have to move away from the farm. It was hard for me to understand because I was only three, and I cried when he told us.

We didn't move too far away so we were able to visit Grandma and Grandpa often. Our new home was nice, but nothing like the farm.

Instead of a pony, we had a toy choo-choo train. My dad had the train track running through the kitchen and around the corner, then it went into the spooky place under the stairs. Next, it went through a tunnel that led into the back porch. When it came back into the kitchen, the whistle would go *toot-toot!* The train made *clickity-clack* sounds as it went on its way. We had a nice backyard with two apple trees and a small garden. When I picked a basket of apples with Mom, I felt important too. I would get to eat one as we worked.

We grew lots of vegetables. Carrots were my favorites. In the summertime, we went on picnics by the Wisconsin River. We saw squirrels, chipmunks, beavers, raccoons, and lots of birds.

When it came time to cut the watermelon, I said, "Oh boy, I want a big piece!"

Mom said, "Don't be a piggy. I'll give you a piece, if you say 'please.'"

She smiled back at me when I said, "May I have some watermelon, please?" I liked watermelon then and still do today.

On one picnic, I took my younger sister, Catherine, to a wild strawberry patch. I was six years old, and she was only three. We put some berries in a little basket and ate a few as we picked. Suddenly, we were ankle-deep in soft mud. It was scary! "Come on, Catherine, let's get out of here!" I hollered. She grabbed my hand as we carefully backed out. I learned what a bog was that day and never went into one again.

Bernard, Catherine, and I went to the playground after our strawberry-picking adventure. The park had swings, teeter-totters, slides, and monkey bars. "Look at me!" I yelled as I quickly climbed up on the bars.

Bernard called out, "You skinny little mosquito."

I said, "You're just jealous because you can't jump around like me."

It was all in good fun, but the nickname stuck, and I liked it. I hopped down and ran over to a swing. I swung really high up into the air. *Wow!* That was a fun day. In the late afternoon, the sun winked at us. Shucks! It was time to go home.

We took our time getting ready for bed that night. First, we brushed our teeth and said good night to everyone, even the dog and the cat. Then we said our prayers. Catherine and I climbed into bed. We talked about our fun time at the park. Bernard yelled from his bedroom, "Hey, you two stop jabbering and go to sleep!" We whispered for a while, but soon my sister was fast asleep.

We were tired from the long, wonderful day. Our little brother, Charlie, was fast asleep in his crib. The house became very quiet. I heard the creaking of the roof as it cooled off from the heat of the day. Mickey, our family dog, was curled up in his basket. Mother Jane, our kitty cat, purred quietly at the foot of our bed. This was a time for dreaming, storing up energy, and getting ready for another summer day. *Zzzzz.*

Mosquito, the Little Girl

Once upon a time, there was a little girl who lived in a quiet small town in Wisconsin. In the summertime, the girl liked to climb trees and roller-skate, among other things. In the winter, there were many outdoor activities: ice-skating and building snowmen and angels in the snow. There were a number of children in the neighborhood, and the spirited girl had fun all year round with her playmates.

One of her favorite games was to tease her older brother, then run for cover. That usually started a great game of hide-and-seek. Because she was so little and quick, her brother called her a mosquito. That name stuck, and she was thereafter called Mosquito. Another favorite pastime was playing with her brother and his miniature locomotive. Their father had the train track running through the kitchen, around the corner, and into the spooky space underneath the stairs and through a tunnel, then out into the back porch. The little train had a whistle that would *toot-toot* as it came *clickity-clack* into the kitchen. What delightful fun!

Springtime was beautiful. All the trees were budding, and the flowers were blooming. Everywhere she went, the small child could smell honeysuckle and lilacs. The garden was a very special place to be when the vegetables were ripe and ready to eat. The carrots were especially tasty when pulled right out of the ground. Strange things grew in that garden, though, like rutabagas, spinach, and turnip! Mosquito didn't know those things would soon show up in one of her mother's soups. She could eat as much as her brother and always have enough room for dessert! No wonder she was so quick; it was all those wonderful things in her mother's soups! Mosquito loved desserts, especially vanilla cream puddings.

In the summertime, there were ice cream socials and many picnics. A favorite treat was vanilla ice cream and Dad's old-fashioned root beer. That was called a "Black Cow." Mosquito's special dessert, well, number two on the list, wasn't the usual chocolate ice cream but orange sherbet. One great big scoop of that and the day was one of the best!

Fourth of July was a great time of the year, with fireworks, music, watermelon, and all sorts of good food. There were parties up and down the street. Families would sit outside at picnic tables, tell stories, and eat some of the best meals one could have. Friends, neighbors, and relatives joined in the festivities, and happy laughter could be heard intermingled with the giggles of children playing.

Summer nights were filled with enchanting entertainment, especially catching fireflies. Catch 'em and put 'em in a Mason quart jar, the lid tight, but already poked with air holes for the little critters. Those neat little insects had a mysterious light on the tip of their tails—fascinating! Mosquito didn't like to keep the fireflies in the jar; she was afraid there wouldn't be any left for the next night, so she let them go. Shucks, the next night, the yard would be alight with those charming little beasties. See, Mosquito did know the best thing to do! The fireflies always came back to her yard, and she knew why.

On hot days, the family would go to the Wisconsin River and play all day. Squirrels, chipmunks, beavers, raccoons, birds, fish, and other wildlife would be everywhere, eating, enjoying the sun, and playing too. The family would have great picnics with lots of good things to eat, especially juicy, ripe watermelon. Neighbors would gather together, and there would be games, boating, fishing, gathering wild berries, and climbing trees, a favorite of the wiry little Mosquito.

On one picnic, Mosquito decided to take her younger sister to a wild strawberry patch and pick some of the best berries around. Suddenly, the girls were ankle-deep in a very soft mud, and it was scary! Their grandmother watched as the two backtracked quickly out of the bog. That was a well-learned lesson. Mosquito never did that again!

The river park had the usual swings, teeter-totter, slides, and monkey bars, plus horseshoe pits for the men. You should have seen that little squirt on the monkey bars! Just like a mosquito flitting here and there. *Wow!* Could she ever move. No wonder the name stuck. When the sun started to sink slowly behind the tree, it was home and off to bed. Jibber-jabber, the two sisters went on and on. Brother thought they would never hush. There were so many interesting things to talk about after hours down by the river. Soon, the warm summer day and all the fun and hard playing caught up with the chattering girls, and all was quiet. Little brother was tucked away in his crib, and big brother was fast asleep.

The house became very quiet. Only the creaking of the roof could be heard as it cooled off from the heat of the day. Mickey, the family dog, was curled up in his basket. Mother Jane, their kitty cat, purred quietly at the foot of the girl's bed. This was time for dreaming, storing up energy, and getting ready for another summer day. *Zzzzz…*

The Man in the Doorway

Boy, listen to that storm! The wind screeched, trees shook, and Halloween was just around the spooky corner! I listened to the tree branches scratching against the window. Or was it really tree branches? More thunder, and lightning snapped across the sky. It was a most scary and noisy night. I tried to count the cracks, booms, and flashes, but there were so many, it was impossible to keep up. *BOOM! CRACK! FLASH! Zip*, under the blankets I went! What was that? Dishes rattled in the kitchen. Who was there? *CRACK!* Rumble, rumble, snap, and more lightning punched the sky. I wondered if it would ever stop.

WHAM! Another thunderclap and lightning. Carefully, I peeked out from under the blankets. It was hard to keep up with all the noise and bright lights.

I thought something was scratching on the floor. It was probably a monster trying to get in and gobble me up! Oh my, what a night! Maybe the scratching noise was a mouse running into its house. It might be scared too. I kept still but tried to find out what was making the strange sound. It could be a Halloween goblin. You must be careful around Halloween. You never know who, or what, is outside in the dark.

Everyone knows that goblins come out late at night to do mischief in your room. Sometimes, they even made a real mess in my dresser drawers. Try to explain that to your mother! Worst of all, they go into the closet and

8

knock clothes off their hangers. They throw one shoe here and the other one who knows where?

It takes fancy words to tell Mother about that. Goblins sneak spinach and broccoli onto your dinner plate too. The nerve of those rascals! You could find muddy footprints in the house all the way from the back porch to your room.

Who put the ring around the bathtub after your bath? The goblins did it!

Oops! I forgot to finish the rest of my story. The thunder rolled across the sky, and bolts of lightning flashed. I listened to creaking tree branches and tall trees groaning in the storm. It was going to be a long night. Scared but sleepy, I hid under the covers for a while. Peeking out into the dark night, I tried to figure out the strange shapes I saw.

Waving shadows danced to and fro. I turned toward the bedroom where my older brother, Bernard, slept. Suddenly, there he was! A man in the doorway! Long arms dangled by his sides, and skinny legs touched the floor. It was dark inside, and I couldn't see his head!

"Mommy! *Mommy!* There's a monster in my room!" It was so spooky, I shivered and shook. I knew it was a monster! After all, only monsters did not have heads! I was certain of that.

Suddenly, the light went on in my room. Mother was standing by my bedside. "What's all the yelling about?" Mom asked. Looking at the door, I saw my monster. Guess what it was? A pair of dad's coveralls hanging from a hook on the door! Did I feel silly!

Feebly, I told Mom what I saw and heard. Mother laughed and said, "You and your wild imagination! What a story to tell Daddy when he comes home from work. Everything is okay. Go back to sleep. When you hear thunder, God is bowling with the angels. They are having fun, and watching over you too."

"It would be quieter if they would play chess, Mom," I answered. "My head always hurts from all the noise. It would be nice to be able to sleep."

I heard the whirr of Dad's car as he drove into the driveway. I felt safe and not afraid anymore. All comfy, I settled down and fell sound asleep. What wonderful dreams I had. But that is a story for another time.

A Walk in the Snow

The sky was dark with snow clouds, and it was cold, but I wanted to go for a walk to visit my friend who lived two houses away. I was three years old that winter.

Mom said, "Come here, and I will help you with your snowsuit and boots. Hold still, you little wiggle worm."

I giggled and said, "But I want to see Beth."

Mom said, "If you want to see her, you have dress up warm to go to her house."

"Okay, Mommy. I will help you to get my boots on. Gee, I look like my teddy bear." In no time at all, I was ready to go out into the winter cold with my snowsuit, boots, mittens, and scarf on.

Mother called my friend's mom and told her I was coming over to play. Beth was my age, and we liked each other. Her mother would wait for me at their house.

The sun peeked out, and it was getting a little warmer. It looked like it would be a good day after all. I waved and started walking down the street. I saw icicles everywhere, and kids making snowmen and snow angels. The trees and bushes were covered with snow. Big snowdrifts covered the cars in the street. It was beautiful. The sun made everything sparkle. I laughed when I made a snowball and threw it at a tree. The tree stood there with its branches hanging down from the weight of the snow looking like a Winter Fairy Princess.

When passing the next-door neighbor's house, I saw their kitty sitting in the window. The kitty's name was Goldie because her fur was golden. She looked at me but went back to cleaning her paw. I called out, "Hi, Goldie."

When she began washing her face, I said, "Bye-bye, Goldie." Goldie held up her little paw. It looked like she was waving to me. I smiled. Goldie was a wise kitty. Did you know that all kitty cats are smart? They know how to get people to care and fuss over them.

Across the street, the neighbor's German shepherd dog played with something in the snow. Not a very bright dog. He didn't even have boots on! Why wasn't he complaining? Oh, how I would cry if my boots weren't on my feet!

My friend's house seemed so far away because of the snow. The sun hid behind the clouds that rolled around the sky.

A giant tree seemed to be waving its branches at me as a cold wind blew them back and forth, snow from its branches falling on the ground as it shook in the wind. I thought that the tree was saying something to me. I froze. It was scary because the tree looked like it might grab me with one of those big branches and eat me up!

Slowly, I turned around and headed home. I began to hurry. Snowflakes fell from the gray clouds. I was very glad to be close to our house because the snowflakes were getting bigger and bigger and coming down faster and faster by the minute!

I ran the rest of the way home. I was out of breath when I climbed the front porch steps. I showed that tree that I could run fast! I felt safe sitting on the porch steps, but a little silly. I knew that trees could not run. I just wanted to be careful.

Mom opened the door and asked, "What are you doing?" Jeepers! My friend's mother had called my mom and told her that I never got to her house.

"Oh, I had to come back because the snow clouds were too big and ugly." I did not want Mom to think I was afraid of my own shadow, or something.

Mom said, "Come inside, and I will help you to take off your snowsuit." While getting out of my warm clothes, I smelled something good.

Oh boy, gingerbread cake with raisins, I guessed. I wanted a glass of milk and a big piece of that cake! Sitting down, I told my mother about the scary things outside. Mom laughed and said, "Oh, you and your wild ideas." The best part of the whole day was that special snack and sitting in my mother's cozy, warm kitchen.

Fire and Ice

Yeeoutch! What was that? It really hurt me! I was sitting on the warm floor vent pulling on my winter socks when a hornet flew up and stung me. That was always a good place to sit, but not that day.

I yelled for Mom. She came into the room and asked, "What's the matter?" I did not want to be called a "cry baby," but I did cry a little. Besides, I wanted to go ice skating with my friends on the frozen Wisconsin River.

Mother looked at my leg and took care of the sting. It did not hurt so much anymore. I was glad about that and could not wait to go outside.

Mother made a nice breakfast of oatmeal with raisins, brown sugar, and milk. Yum-yum! That was a fine way to start the day. I liked winter, with lots of snow and shiny icicles everywhere. We had many fun things to do, like ice skating, skiing, making snowmen and snow angels, and throwing snowballs.

I was all dressed, then Mom helped me into my snowsuit and boots. I was ready for a fun time. Out the door I went to play with my friends.

The shining sun always made it warm and pretty outside. The snow sparkled so brightly, it made me blink. It was so beautiful, and I was happy. Holding my skates, I walked down the street, kicking up the snow. Poof! The snow flew off my boot. I did it again—it was fun! Lots of people were already ice-skating on the river. Everyone was having fun. After putting on my skates, I raced onto the ice. I liked to skate fast!

Suddenly, I heard the sound of ice cracking! I was on thin ice, and I wanted to get off! I jumped up, spun around, and quickly skated back to my friends. My brother saw what happened and said, "Boy, did you look funny!" That was enough. I decided to skate another time when the ice was more frozen. I took off my skates and pulled on my boots. I walked the short way home. Mom asked, "Why are you home so soon?"

"The river wasn't frozen enough for skating, so some of us quit," I said.

Looking out the window, I watched the sun sparkle on the snow. It was warmer, and I wondered what I wanted to do next. Beautiful rainbows made the icicles look like Christmas lights. There were big snowdrifts in the backyard. I could go skiing! At six years old, all I thought about was skiing on my "mountains." Piles of snow had drifted against the fences in everyone's yard. I could ski all around our neighborhood.

Outside, Dad said, "Okay, let's get your skis ready. I'll make sure they are on correctly." I pushed off with my ski poles. *Whoosh! Whoosh! Whoosh!* You could hear me as I skied across the backyards. Seeing my neighbors, I shouted, "Hello." I even yelled hello to the neighbors' dogs as I passed them. That was a lot of fun, and good exercise too. No wonder I was a healthy little girl!

After the last turn, I was getting tired. Glad to see our house, I skied softly to the porch. Dad helped me take off my skis.

He said, "Your cheeks look like rosy apples." I said, "It was fun. The snow was high everywhere." I was tired from the day of skating and skiing—it was super.

After dinner, I brushed my teeth to get ready for an early bedtime. I had trouble keeping my eyes open. Mother tucked me in bed and said, "You can play in the snow tomorrow too." I am sure I fell asleep with a smile on my face. You can bet that my dreams were all about snowmen and snow angels.

The Old Barn at the farm at Arnott, WI, still standing
when this picture was taken in 1986

Varmints under the Porch

Here is a secret I will share with you. One day, I decided that I wanted a spoonful of sugar. Oh my, that sugar did taste good! I got up on a chair and then onto our table. At three years old, I was quite a climber. Uh-oh! Someone was coming into the kitchen. I quickly got down and sneaked out the back door to the front yard.

I had a secret hideout under the house. Squeezing through a space, I crawled into my fort. It was nice and warm in there, and I was happy. Our kitty followed me in and purred. We called our cat Mother Jane because she was always good to us. Kitty liked to curl up with us on the sofa, our beds, or our laps. It felt good to have such lovely company. Our kitty was friendly, and she had an all-white coat. She had kittens that were two weeks old. I did not worry about that because she was on my lap. She let me play with her long tail. I told her, "You are a good kitty, Mother Jane." She purred like a motor boat. "Nice kitty, good kitty," I said. I hoped that she would stay with me until it was safe to come out. Mother Jane had other ideas. She stretched, looked up at me, rubbed her soft face on my arm, and went out.

Omigosh! My furry friend slipped away and left me under the house! Oh well, I found some sticks and stones to make a tiny fort. Suddenly, I heard footsteps. Mom called me. The way she said made me think that I get hurt. Always tell me where you are." Guess what? I did not get sent to my room. Mother was happy that I was all right. Dad said, "You don't like it under the house anymore? You sure came out in a hurry this time."

18

"There was something under there with beady eyes. I didn't like that at all," I said.

Dad said, "Probably varmints. They are just plain old rats and not friendly like our kitty."

He helped me understand why I should never go anywhere without telling Mom. Mother took me into the kitchen. I got more hugs and kisses. That was so nice.

Then I sat down, and she gave me a bowl of warm vanilla pudding. Yum, yum! I learned my lesson that day. Never steal a spoonful of sugar and hide under the house. Mom hummed a song as she worked in her kitchen. Mother Jane sat on the floor purring. "Mommy, thank you for the pudding. It's really good," I said. Mom smiled and said, "You're welcome." That was quite a day.

Mack's Crossing

We moved to Winslow, Arizona, when I was seven years old. *Oh my gosh*! What a change from Stevens Point, Wisconsin! Dad took us to some really cool places. One of our favorite places in Arizona was Mack's Crossing. It is on East Clear Creek up in the White Mountains. I liked the mountains because the pine trees were so tall. I could climb on top of big rocks or play in the water. It smelled so nice in the high mountains. One time, Dad was took us to Mack's Crossing to spend the weekend camping.

I got up early one morning as the sun smiled brightly in the clear blue sky. "Wake up, Catherine," I told my sister. "We get to go to the mountains today."

"Leave me alone. I'm still sleepy, Carlene." Sleepyhead was four years old at the time.

"*Oh phooey!* You can sleep in the car!"

Sis grumbled but got up. We dressed and then went into the kitchen.

"Look, Mommy made pancakes and bacon. Pancakes always wakes you up, sis," I informed her. After eating breakfast, we were ready to go.

My older brother, Bernard, helped Dad put our picnic basket, water, and fishing poles in the car. The tent was tied to the top of the car. Dad was driving, and Mom sat next to him. My baby brother, Charlie, was on her lap. Bernard, Catherine, and I were in the back seat. Our dog, Mickey, curled up next to me. I said, "Catherine, sit on my lap so you can see out of the window better." I hugged her. "Oh, you are so cute."

I was thinking about the wild animals and hoped that we would see some of them. I knew about snakes, squirrels, chipmunks, coyotes, wolves, mountain lions, deer, bears, and lots of birds too. The fish were fun to watch as they swam in the clear mountain streams. Some of the fish with brown dots on them are called brown trout, and some with beautiful rainbows on their sides are called rainbow trout.

We started so early that it was not just Catherine who had fallen asleep—all of us kids fell asleep. *Shhh!* Someone was stirring in the back seat. Mosquito was awake! I yawned and asked, "Where are we?" Dad said, "We are about halfway to the crossing. How are you doing?"

"Okay," Bernard and I answered. Catherine was still sleeping next to me and Mickey. Soon we were driving higher and higher into the mountains. Catherine woke up and looked out the window. She said, "There goes a big rabbit under that bush." Dad made a turn and said, "We are going down into the canyon now, so roll up the windows so the dust won't fly in." We did that right away.

"Catherine, look, the creek! Down there!" I pointed. The sun winked at us between the trees. Best of all, the sun made beautiful colors dance upon the water. The big cottonwood trees looked like they were waving at us.

"Listen to that bird, Bernard. It sure is noisy! *Chirp, chirp, chirp*," I went, trying to sound like the bird.

"Yeah, it sure is noisy—just like you, squirt." We all laughed as I continued to chirp away, pretending to be talking to the birds as we drove along.

"Look, quick!" Catherine said. "Over there! A squirrel is running up that tree! It's so cute." She pointed to a tall pine tree off to the left of us. The furry little animal stopped to watch us go by with its pretty eyes and its bushy tail going *swish, swish*.

"There are more squirrels on that big tree, Catherine. They are collecting nuts to store for the winter." I felt important because I was teaching my sister something.

Catherine squealed, "Over there. I see some deer behind that big boulder!"

"They are pretty. One has antlers on its head," Mom said. "Remember, the one with the antlers is a male deer, and the other one without antlers is called a doe, a female deer."

The deer munched on some soft, green grass as we drove away. That was something to talk about to our friends at home.

On and on we went, never a dull moment. Sometimes, an animal would dart out ahead of us as we drove, but we could not clearly see what it was. We heard snaps and crackling sounds in the bushes that were hiding whatever animal had jumped into them.

I always asked, "What was that? Jeepers, isn't this a great place to live? I could stay up here in the mountains, and no one would know I was here."

"Go ahead, move up here anytime you want, and then we wouldn't have to listen to you, Miss Chatterbox," Bernard said.

"You wouldn't miss me?" I asked.

"Yeah, I would miss you, squirt. You sure can play great baseball! Our friends need you on our side because you can hit the baseball a country mile!"

"I sure can, and I run fast too!" That was true because I was a real outdoor girl, and not afraid to work or play hard.

I sat by the window with my nose pressed against it. We had traveled awhile, and the road seemed like it would never end. We were all quiet. "Carlene, what are you thinking?" Mom asked.

"This sure is a long way home, Mom. There are more animals and birds going up this side too."

Catherine giggled and said, "I like the little squirrels and the deer."

"How much longer do we have to drive before we reach the highway?" Mom asked Dad.

"We're over halfway there, and the road is good. We're making good time, Mother. We'll be home in time for dinner, so don't worry," Dad replied.

"What are those wide spaces along the road, Dad?" I asked.

"Those are picnic spots."

There were more birds flying in the air and lots of squirrels on the ground and in the trees. I saw some animal run into the bushes, but I couldn't tell what it was for certain.

Bernard said, "Look at that big bird over there. It's an eagle. It sure is watching us. Probably wants some food. There's the campground and the creek!"

The water flowed lazily around the giant rocks and past the tall trees. Sunbeams twinkled through the trees, reflecting on the windshield as Dad drove up and parked. He picked a spot to put up our tent, which was made of heavy brown canvas. It had long poles standing inside to keep it from falling down. Dad put long stakes in the ground and tied the tent ropes to them. He and my brother put the poles inside the tent and stood them up straight. That was a big job. "Yes, but let me get them started, then you won't hit your hands." That was fun, and I did not even hurt myself! The tent was nine feet wide and twelve feet long. We were proud of it.

While Mom was getting lunch ready, Catherine and I had our job to do: We picked up small pine tree branches and put them on the tent floor. Bernard brought in canvas tarps (like blankets) and said, "Grab this end and take it to the top." We put two of those down so that the branches were all covered. Then we put pillows and blankets on top of them so we would be comfy at night.

Mom called, "Lunch is ready!" We had sandwiches, soda pop, and big red apples. After lunch, Dad reached into his fishing basket and said, "I've got a surprise for you, kids. Close your eyes and put out your hands." We all did as Dad told us to. I squealed, "A Babe Ruth candy bar! *Wow!* Thanks, Daddy, my favorite!"

The three of us went to the crossing to dangle our feet in the water. Catherine said, "*Brrr*, it's cold, but it feels good." The cool water did feel nice on a hot summer day. We all laughed when Catherine said, "A fish just touched my foot, and it tickled!" I bent down and touched one on its tail. *Whoosh!* The fish swam off in a big hurry. "Don't splash me, Carlene," Catherine said.

"Okay, but let's have some fun," I said. We stood up and kicked the water, making big waves for a while until we were tired. Then we sat down on the bank, exhausted and wet from head to toe.

"Catherine, look! I caught a fish with my hands!" It quickly wiggled out of my grip, dropped down into the water, and swam away. It was a beautiful rainbow trout.

Dad came over and said, "I'm going fishing upstream with Bernard. You girls mind your mother."

"Yes, Daddy. Catch some big ones!" I said. As we waved, I knew that we would have trout for dinner that night.

Catherine went to sit by Mom and asked for a story. I had an idea. "Mom, may I go watch Dad and Bernard fish?"

"Yes, but let Daddy know when you get there. Walk on the path and don't go into the water."

"Okay, Mom. I know the way, and no water play," I answered.

The flowers were pretty in the mountains, and it was very peaceful. While walking, I remembered seeing a meadow full of sheep earlier. There they were! The sheep were munching on the green grass. I stopped to watch them for a while. I skipped, hopped, and sang like the birds as I went along the path. I saw Dad and my brother as I went around a bend. "Hey, I'm here! Mom said I could come up. Did you catch any fish yet?"

"I caught one, and Dad got two," Bernard said.

"Yummy, we're going to have fish for dinner," I said. I climbed on top of a big rock to watch them fish. It was easy because I liked to climb. "This is a great place up here, Dad. I can see both of you and some fish in the water. Hey, I can see lots of birds, and there's a beaver!"

"*SHHH!*" Dad and Bernard said.

"Okay, I'll be quiet." I watched them and listened to the birds. It was a great place to sit and see so much.

After a while, Dad said they had caught enough for all of us for dinner. Shucks, time to go. I slid down off the big rock and landed in soft sand. Whew, that was fun! I ran to Dad and looked into his fishing basket.

"Wow, Dad, those fish are big! Nice dinner tonight, right?"

"Yep," Bernard added proudly.

I sang, skipped, and bounced around like a little bunny rabbit as we headed back to camp. I knew my way and ran ahead. I waited behind a big tree until Dad and my brother got closer. "Boo! I bet I scared you!"

"You're a goofball," Bernard said.

I laughed and said, "I'm a fast goofball!" I ran ahead of them to be the first one back at camp to tell Mom the news.

"Mom, Bernard and Dad got lots of nice fish! I climbed on top of a big rock to watch them. It was beautiful and quiet up there."

"Yeah, after we told the chatterbox to hush!" Bernard said as he and Dad walked into the campsite just behind me. Mom had potatoes baking in the firepit and corncobs boiling in a big kettle. Dad had the fish ready for Mom to fry. In a few minutes, we would be eating. "I'll get the soda pop, Mom." I ran to the creek and took out a few cans. "Whew, these are cold, just like we want them," I said.

"Let's wash the dishes, Catherine, so Mom can tell us a story." We put all the dirty things in a basket and went to the creek. The water bubbled and made little splashes against the rocks. A few fish swam by as we worked. "This is a fun way to clean the plates, Carlene," Catherine said. Everything was quickly stored away when we gave the clean dishes to Mom. We sat on a log and watched the fire wink and spit out sparks as Mom got ready to tell us a story.

Before she could begin speaking, a sound not too far away from our camp made me and my sister jump. *Yip, yip, yip!* "The coyotes are out hunting," Dad said. We were used to the wild animals in Arizona, but they still sounded spooky. After a long day playing in the mountain air and sunshine, we were getting sleepy earlier than usual. It was not even dark yet. Mom said, "Get ready for bed, kids." There was not much to do except brush our teeth and put on our pajamas. We crawled under the blankets. I chatted to Catherine, but I looked at her and knew that I was talking to myself. I giggled and cuddled up to her.

That night, I'd have nice dreams of trout swimming in the streams and eagles flying in the air. We were going to leave in the late afternoon the next day.

I collected some pretty rocks, pine cones, leaves, and some bird feathers to show my friends at home. I put all my precious things in a basket Mom had given me.

The Long Ride Home

In the morning, Dad said, "On our way home from the crossing, we will go up the other side of the canyon. The road goes through a forest, so keep a sharp eye out for animals."

"Oh boy, that's great. I bet we will see coyotes and deer," Bernard said.

"Maybe. Just keep looking," Dad said.

"When will we get home?" I asked.

"About the same time we usually do, late afternoon," Dad said as he drove slowly over the big, flat rocks of the crossing. The water wasn't deep, but our car made ripples, splashes, and little waves as we headed up the other side.

"*Shhh!* Catherine, listen! You can hear the water singing a pretty song," I said. Catherine was sitting on my lap trying to hear it, looking so serious with her head tilted to one side and her face concentrating hard. We were on an old, dirt road that was wide and not too bumpy. It twisted and turned as we passed giant trees and big rocks. However, as we climbed the mountain, it got colder.

Catherine asked, "Help me put my sweater on, please." It took just a minute to put it over her head and pull down.

"Okay, do you feel warmer now?" I asked.

"Uh-huh." She nodded.

"*Wow!* That was fun going up and down that hill," I said.

Sis giggled, "It made my tummy tickle!"

"Look quick," Dad said. "An animal just ran into the bushes over on the right."

"Oh, phooey," I said. "I couldn't see exactly what it was. It was all furry and looked like a big dog. It had a bushy tail and pointy ears."

Mom asked, "What do you think it was, Carlene? Remember all the animals we talked about on the way up the canyon road?"

Before my brother could answer, I shouted, "A coyote! I bet it was a coyote!" I had seen pictures of wild animals in school, and I knew that had to be a coyote! *Wow!* This is a fun trip!

On and on Dad drove, uphill and then downhill on the road. Bernard laughed when we went over a big bump. "This road is better for goats than for cars, Dad," he said.

"Uh-oh!" Dad said as he slowed down to a complete stop.

I said, "Look at that! There's a big tree lying right on the road!" Dad got out of the car and took an ax out of the trunk. It was too far to go back to the crossing to go home.

The tree had to be moved. He started chopping on the dead, rotten tree. When he stepped on it, some pieces fell to the ground. I got out and walked on the tree too. It felt squishy, like a pile of leaves. It was a very tall tree.

"Oh, look at the bugs! There are cute little furry caterpillars, ants, black beetles, and nice worms that we could use for fishing," I said. Dad and Bernard took turns chopping the tree. My brother was almost twelve years old, and he was tall and strong.

I asked, "Daddy, can I chop too?" He gave me a smaller ax while he and Bernard rested. My father had taught us how to use an ax at home, so I was careful and felt important. That year, I was almost nine and full of energy too. "It is hard work chopping, and now I need a rest," I said. We cleared the road, but it took a lot of time.

The sun peeked through the trees. Soft breezes brushed our skin. From high above we heard *Who, who-who, whooo?* It was an owl talking to its friends. The trees were whispering to each other. Shadows were creeping around, and the birds were getting quiet.

I said, "I bet the trees are saying, 'Silly people on that old road, and the sun doing down soon for the night.'"

"We are going to be home late tonight," Dad said to us all.

"Boy, I will be glad to be in my own bed," I groaned. Catherine and my baby brother, Charlie, were already fast asleep.

Finally, Dad and Bernard had cleared away enough of the old tree for us to drive through and be on our way back home. We were still on the forest road, but finally we were getting closer to the highway. We could see car lights snaking along the road. But before we could reach the highway, Dad said, "The bridge over the wash is out. Must have been a cloudburst out here, but the wash is dry now." No sign or anything! Just *no* bridge!

It was getting darker by the minute. Dad drove alongside the wash, checking for a safe place to cross. Oh my, the tires whirred and whizzed as he carefully inched the car across a shallow place. The road was much better on the other side as we finally made it down and up the other side of the dry creek bed. "Yippee! I can see the town lights!" I said. "Look at the moon. It's so bright! But the desert without the light looks scary at night." Cactus, big rocks, and bushes looked like animals in the dark. But in our car, I felt safe because we were together and getting closer to our home.

It was after midnight when we finally pulled into our driveway. Mom said, "Kids, brush your teeth, put on your pajamas, and go to bed." We didn't fuss about that.

Mom tucked us in bed, and soon it was quiet. Tomorrow we would talk about our camping trip. It was the longest nineteen-mile-drive from the mountains down to our home in Winslow, out in the desert of Arizona. My bed never felt so comfy and warm as it did that night.

The Rattlesnake Hunt

Rattlesnakes! Tomorrow was the big day. My brother and I were going rattlesnake hunting! Everything was ready. We had been planning our outing carefully now for over a week. My brother was going on fourteen, and I was ten years old. Dad had taught us about gun safety, and we knew how to handle them. I was glad we listened to him.

Arizona was fun. There was always something to do. We got up before sunrise, and in no time, the campfire was red hot, and sparks flew out as we made our cowboy breakfast. The bacon sputtered and cooked quickly. The fried eggs looked nothing like Mom's, but we ate them anyway. The beans and coffee were not the best, either. We ate, and when we had our fill, we dumped the leftover coffee on the fire and smothered it with sand to make sure it was completely out.

"Okay, Carlene, check our list to be sure that we have everything," Bernard said.

"Had breakfast, fire out, washed the dishes, bicycles ready, gun set to go. Perfect checkoff," I answered smartly.

"Okay, let's fill these jugs with water then tie them to our bicycles," Bernard said. The night before, my brother had told Mom we were going for a bike ride in the early morning.

She said, "Okay, you two be careful, and remember to take water with you." Hopping on our trusty "horses"—our bikes—we rode out. It was too

early to worry about the coyotes, but we knew that snakes liked the warm sunshine.

"Hey, look at the desert rose growing out of that rock," I said. It was pretty. The sunrise was beautiful. It was good that we left early. Hawks, ravens, and vultures flew high above. I wondered how it was possible for them to survive out there. The lizards were fun to watch as they ran across rocks and under bushes. One stood on top of a big rock, stared at us, then jumped down. It stuck out its tongue at us as it ran away.

We reached a place where my brother figured rattlesnakes were hiding in their caves, called lairs. "Look, a snake just wiggled under that bush!" Bernard said. We had seen snakes in museums, but this was different.

I did not want to stare into a rattlesnake's home. I kept a safe distance away from the hole. "Stand back, and don't move an inch," Bernard yelled. BANG! The shot rang out. *Wow!* He made certain that the snake was dead. The snake had crawled halfway under a bush. Bernard had shot the rattles off it and pulled them close to him with a big stick. He counted nine rings on the rattle.

One of our Navajo friends once told Bernard, "Never shoot a rattlesnake for fun, and never trust it to be dead either." That was good advice.

When we got home, Mom was baking bread. It smelled wonderful. We put our "horses" into the shed and went inside. "Where have you two been?" Mom asked.

Bernard answered, "On a bike ride, remember? We talked about it yesterday. We saw a great sunrise."

"It must have been a long ride. Go clean up. You two are dusty-looking."

We had cold lemonade and hot bread with butter and strawberry jam. Yummy! Looking at the rattles, Mom asked, "Where did you get that thing?"

"Oh, it was lying around. I like it," Bernard said. Mom did not say anything. I was too busy eating fresh bread to speak.

Tomorrow was another day, and who knows what we would think of to do. The next day, we went to the schoolyard to show our friends what we had. It was summertime, and kids came there to play every day. Bernard proudly showed off the rattle to his friends and all the other boys who wanted to look at the large rattle. My girlfriend Susan asked, "Icky, where did you get the rattle? Weren't you afraid? What are you going to do with it?"

Bernard said, "I had a special reason to kill the rattlesnake. I'm going to be part of something important. I can't tell you anymore."

"How come I wasn't told about it?" I asked. I was hurt because he had left me out of whatever it was he was planning to do. That was not fair; he always included me in on everything. At least I thought so.

Special or not, I never did find out what the big fuss was about. I did learn that Bernard was invited to spend a whole day with some of our Navajo friends. No one ever shared a cotton-pickin' thing about that day with me.

"Bernard, when are you going to tell me what you did with that rattle?" I asked one day.

"*Never!* I can't tell you anything," he said, and he was serious. I grumbled about that for a few days, but it never did me any good. Drats!

Heinz, the All-American Miceologist

Gotcha! Caught something good again! Heinz, the cat, was happy with her mouse. But she was thinking about going to America. She lived in Canberra, Australia, with her American family. Heinz loved her family, even though she had lived with them for just a few years.

One day, strange things began to happen. Her family was excited and very busy. Friends and neighbors visited their home. The telephone rang and rang. Heinz wondered what was going on. Poor kitty. It was confusing. Heinz followed everyone around, trying to figure out what the fuss was all about.

Someone talked about moving and sending things back to the States. Did they mean the United States? Oh no! What about me? She hoped to go to America too.

She did not know if the family planned to take her along. Heinz thought about how to find a way to get to the United States and study American "Miceology." Heinz would think about that later. Right now, it was catnap time. *Purrrrr.*

Later, one of the children picked Heinz up and gave her a big hug. Heinz opened her sleepy eyes and looked around the room. Everyone was happy. The girl said, "Heinz, you are going to America with us!"

"Meow, meow." Heinz was happy too. Two weeks later, Heinz was placed in her kitty carrier, and the family went to the Canberra airport.

They boarded a small airplane called a "puddle jumper"—the type of plane that makes short trips.

With a high-pitched *whirr* that settled down to a steady VROOM, the plane lifted off and flew high into the blue sky. Heinz curled up in her carrier next to one of the girls. Poor kitty was too scared to purr, and her tummy made funny noises. *Oh my*, Heinz thought. *I do not like this airplane stuff at all.* The plane took them from Canberra to the big city of Sydney, Australia. When they landed, someone took Heinz off the plane.

I can see my family so I must be all right, Heinz thought. Soon, Heinz's carrier was picked up again. She looked out of her little window in the front of the carrier as she was taken by the attendant to a bigger airplane to be with her family.

Inside the big jumbo jet, they all settled down in their seats. Heinz stretched and purred. Soon, she was sound asleep.

The big jet took off, and up they flew into the blue sky again. They went to a faraway place called the Fiji islands. They had to stop there because the airplane needed fuel, and the people were hungry. Heinz did not want any food as her tummy was still acting funny from the flight. Finally, back aboard, the jet took off again.

It was a long time until the jet landed again, this time in a beautiful place called Honolulu, Hawaii.

Everyone got off the plane. One of the girls opened Heinz's carrier and hooked a leash to her collar. What did that mean? Kitty looked around and was happy to see her family. She got to walk and smell the fresh air. Heinz tweaked her little black nose and sniffed at everything. She thought how nice it was here.

The children's mother bought a picnic lunch. They ate in the warm sunshine. Soon lunch was over—including a little lunch for Heinz this time—and Heinz was soon back in her carrier.

They got aboard another big jet. *How many more airplanes do I have to fly to get where we are going to in America?* thought Heinz. Their last stop was Seattle, Washington. America! We're finally here! It had taken thirty-one hours to fly from Canberra to Seattle. The children were tired of being cooped up for so long. The plane landed, and in a few minutes, they left the aircraft.

Their mother said, "Kids, we are home at last." Heinz hoped that she would never have to fly in a plane again. All she wanted to do was begin her new life and learn about American "Miceology." She purred and thought about how lucky she was and how special it was to be here. She sat inside her carrier like a furry little princess and purred.

Sergeant Nick, Guard Dog Extraordinaire

(A Fictional Story of a Beloved Dog)

"Mommy! Mommy! Wake up! You said that today we are going to get our puppy, remember?" Brother Jimmy was as excited as he always was on Christmas morning. Mommy opened her sleepy eyes.

Little sister Cathy tugged at the blankets and squealed, "Puppy, Mommy, puppy!"

Mother fixed breakfast, cleaned up the kitchen, and said, "Let's go now, okay?" Everyone piled into Mom's car, and off they went. It was a good day to look for a puppy.

In her hand, their mother held a newspaper advertisement about six schnoodle puppies for sale. She said, "I'm not sure what a schnoodle is. It sounds more like something good to eat." Cathy giggled at the funny name, and kept saying it over and over until she finally got tired.

They found the house at the address listed in the newspaper. The children were very excited. Jimmy knocked on the door and heard lots of sounds going *yap-yap, woof-woof!*

"I hope they are fine little dogs, but what a silly name, schnoodles."

A lady opened the door and said, "Hello, did you come to look at the puppies? They are a schnauzer and poodle mix, and all of them are brown and white."

Jimmy said, "Can we see them now? I want to know what they look like."

"Okay, just follow me. My name is Sally. The puppies are out in the backyard."

"I'm June," Mom said. "This is Jimmy and Cathy. We are looking for our first dog."

Sally opened the back door, and the children followed her.

The puppies were running and tumbling all over each other. They ran to the children and crowded around them, jumping and wagging their tails. Jimmy picked up one that caught his eye and looked at his mother. "Can I have this one, Mommy, please?" The furry little animal stuck his nose into Jimmy's shirt pocket, and then it licked him on the cheek. Jimmy giggled. Cathy said, "Me too, want puppy!" Jimmy sat down on the ground so that Cathy could pet their new friend.

Their mother paid Sally for the puppy while the children played with it. Off they went into Mom's car, happy to have a puppy of their own. She put the children in their car seats. The small ball of fur went safely into his new doggie carrier. Jimmy said, "We need a name for our puppy. Let's think about one." Jimmy and his sister thought of Scooter, Jason, Lucky, and Mickey.

That was a lot of work, and it wore them out. Cathy fell asleep. Jimmy sat quietly with his thinking cap on. He looked serious. No one agreed on a name that night. It was serious business to name a dog. They had to get it just right.

The next morning, the children were playing with the puppy in their backyard. They were having fun laughing and running around.

The dog was barking in his little puppy yips and woofs. Jimmy's friends, Nicholas and Joey, came over. Nicholas said, "I heard a puppy yipping and yapping. Gee, it's cute. What's its name?"

"I got it!" Jimmy yelled. I am going to name our puppy Nicholas!" Everyone thought that was a great idea, especially Nicholas.

The puppy grew fast the first year and became a great guard dog. Each day, he would march all along the fence in the backyard. He would stop every now and then to look around and sniff the air. Then he continued on his patrol. He always barked at the birds and airplanes. Never did one land in his yard! He kept everyone out who did not belong there. What a brave dog, and he weighed just twelve and a half pounds when he was fully grown. Nicholas, guard dog extraordinaire!

Good Morning

Good morning, good morning!
The sun is on the rise.
The moon is hiding behind the skies
as the morning glory opens her sleepy eyes.
Little birdies chirp loudly on high
while squirrels scamper all around.
A beautiful butterfly lands aground
and whispering breezes so softly sound.
Good morning, good morning!
My little one greets the day.
Here comes the sun to lead the way
as sparkling dewdrops kiss the hay.

The Whistling Bird

Come 'round, little children
and listen to my song.
I am the whistler you have heard so long.
I whistle and sing to every new day
and do hope you hear what I have to say.

Birdie Delight

"Ha, ha, ha!" said the birdie in the tree.
I am hungry, and I like what I see!
Your apple so round and so sweet,
If only it would fall at my feet!

The Bee

I'm a little bee
Buzzing in the clover.
Oh, please, Mrs. Cow,
Do step over!

Piggy

Piggy, piggy in the pen.
How many times have you
Sounded like a hen?
Look around and you will see
Just who the piggy
Seems to be.

Plinkity-Plank

Plinkity-plank, give a yank.

Jump up and down and call for Hank!

Now push a button, ring-a-ling.

Let's all have fun, and sing and sing.

What can we do to be so kookie?

Just see here now and lookie lookie.

Why plinkity-plank, give a yank.

Jump up and down and call for Hank!

51

My Choo-Choo

I have a little choo-choo.
It huffs and puffs along the street.
Down the winding railroad track
and up the grassy knoll.
I like to sing and dance for joy
when I hear it chug-a-lug.
It seems to sing along with me
as I watch it go along merrily.

Reflections

Teddy bears and ribbons
And lace do I have.
Dollies and dancers
And wee little gnomes all
Surround me in my little home.
The sweetest reflections
Of life do I own.

The Owie

I had an owie that hurt so bad.
Into the car I went with my dad.
To see my doctor we did go.
I was so brave, you couldn't know.
The nurse asked, "Now where does it hurt?"
I hoped my answer did not sound curt.
Way down in my tummy so very low,
It felt like a thorn from a thistletoe.
In came my doctor to check me out.
"Looks like the flu without a doubt."
Home I went with a bottle of pills.
Oh my gosh, I'll be stuffed to the gills!
"No," Mommy said, "only one at a time."
Oh, thank heavens, now isn't that fine?
In a few days, I'll be all better. I guess
I'll send my doc a thank-you letter.

Halloween

Pumpkins and apples
And ghosts out on a prowl.
You see them all one night
While the cold wind howls.
Goblins and monsters now do I hear,
As I hide under the blankets on
The spookiest day of the year.

Little Things

Tweaking, stretching, and wiggling my toes
I found myself looking for little things
As I walked along the seashore in the sun
On a beautiful, warm summer day.
So many wonderful seashells did I see.
I gathered my treasures and put them away.
The seagulls soon came to see what I had.
I'm sorry to say I had nothing for them today.
Over the waves floated a lovely flower.
What an interesting discovery to arrive that way.
Curiosity struck me as I studied my find
While high above floated laughing, white clouds.
My day at the beach was ever so pleasant.
I collected, examined, and stored all my pretties.
Soon the sun was setting over the sea,
And slowly, I drifted away to dream of another day.

Shadows of the Night

Two by the river and one down by the old
banyan tree.
Always waiting and watching and never a
sound will you hear.
Moving ever so quietly with only the stars
plotting their path.
I marveled at their quiet confidence and
swaying way.
Under the moonlight and beneath the
lovely shrubs of green.
Now down by the waterfall, now gracefully
over the rim.
High on a lofty perch way up in a tree,
A wise old owl hoots knowingly to all
below.
Shadows of the night wait, and watch for
first morning light.

My mother, Margaret Irene (née Schulfer) Maciejewski, on her wedding day at the farmhouse in Arnott, WI. September 28, 1933.

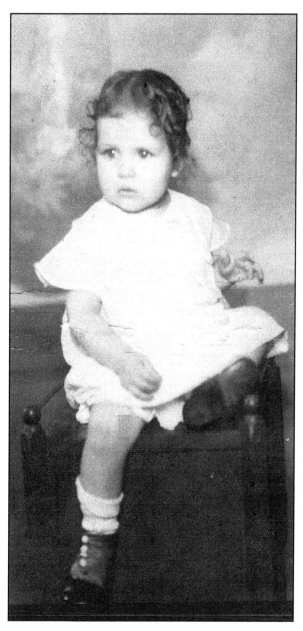

Me, the author, Carlene A. (née Maciejewski) Lanier, about two years old.

The author when she and her husband, Jim, lived at Ocen Shores, WA. Little "Sergeant Nick" is on the ground to the left in the picture.

About the Author

Carlene A. Lanier discovered her passion for writing in the fifth grade. She enjoys working on her memoirs, short stories, children's fiction, and poetry. Mrs. Lanier and her husband, Jim, raised four wonderful and successful children: James, Teresa, Ceit, and Elizabeth. As a psychiatric registered nurse, she worked in hospitals, clinics, drug treatment facilities, and community mental health centers. She lives in Arizona with her husband and their Shih Tzu, Sophie.

CPSIA information can be obtained
at www.ICGtesting.com
Printed in the USA
JSHW071241020623
42629JS00005B/56

9 781684 980208